THE ETERNAL OLD LADY
BANK OF ENGLAND HISTORY & DEVELOPMENT

Ian Moncrief-Scott

Information Management Solutions Limited

ISLE OF MAN

The author Ian Moncrief-Scott has asserted his right under the Copyright, Designs and Patents Act 1988 to be identified as the author of this work.

Copyright. © I. Moncrief-Scott 2021

All rights reserved. No part of this publication may be produced in any form or by any means - graphic, electronic, or mechanical, including photocopying, recording, taping, or information storage and retrieval systems - without the prior permission in writing of the publishers.

The publishers make no representation, express or implied, regarding the accuracy of the information contained in this book and cannot accept any legal responsibility for any errors or omissions that may take place.

A CIP catalogue record for this book is available from the British Library.

Published by Information Management Solutions Limited, 17 Howe Road, Onchan, Isle of Man, IM3 2BB.

Printed, bound and distributed by IngramSpark.

Book Layout © 2017 BookDesignTemplates.com

Superhero Peg Image: Besjunior/Shutterstock.com

Cover Source by Tanja Prokop of BookDesignTemplates.com

THE ETERNAL OLD LADY: BANK OF ENGLAND HISTORY & DEVELOPMENT – 2nd ed.
ISBN 9781903467060

The Publishers have been requested by the author to acknowledge the direct and indirect contributions to this book by The Bank of England.

This book is dedicated to
start-up entrepreneurs.

The front cover depicts
ordinary wooden clothes pegs dressed as
Super Heroes.

**All start-up entrepreneurs are
ordinary people
turning into Super Heroes!**

CONTENTS

THE ETERNAL OLD LADY 1
BIBLIOGRAPHY 9
OTHER BOOKS BY THE AUTHOR 11
FORCOMING BOOKS BY THE AUTHOR 13

THE ETERNAL OLD LADY

War created the Bank of England.

Had King William III possessed enough money to combat France's Louis X1V, the first public bank may have never emerged. According to his statue in the magnificent Hall of the Bank, the King is credited with founding the formidable institution, but a commoner,

William Paterson first conceived the Old Lady.

With a more trusted Government, a less reckless previous monarch and properly accounted state money, the Bank would have been unimaginable.

Money lending was ancient. Discounting bills of exchange went back to the 12th century.

In London, goldsmiths paid interest on deposits. Scriveners (solicitors' mortgage clerks) raised funds. Merchants, brokers, usurers and discounters of bills and tallies operated routinely. Joint Stock Companies like Sword Mills Company and Mine Adventurers issued notes and lent money on securities.

These independent activities converged with cheque payments between 1830-1870. Note issue was the last classical banking function to evolve in England and contributed significantly to today's European banking system.

City of London Bank failed in 1682. National Bank of Credit folded a year later. Daring proposals were needed for a public bank.

In 1687, the first treasure was salvaged from a Spanish ship lost 40 years earlier in Hispaniola. Investors returned 10,000% profit -20% of the entire national revenue. Despite war by the Grand Alliance against France, over 150 treasure hunting companies and the new stock exchange inspired an economic miracle.

Ironically, William Paterson was a Scot. Born in Dumfriesshire, he travelled to America to seek his fate. Some say he became a buccaneer, others a missionary. Fact reveals that he worked for London's Merchant Tailors Company. He journeyed to the West Indies and visited both Hamburg and Amsterdam, two pinnacles of banking.

Paterson formed a company in 1691 to lend His Majesty's Government £1 million at 6% annual interest with a £5000 management fee. The offer was rejected. His second proposal, a £2 million loan, was similarly scorned.

Charles Montagu tried to fill the Exchequer void with a Lottery loan. It failed miserably. Paterson was again invited. This time, powerful Whig merchants and the City of London supported the venture.

Paterson, also noted for the flawed Darien Adventure, an attempt to colonise the Panama Isthmus that gorged half of Scotland's wealth was joined by Sir John Houblon, a subsequent Lord Mayor of London.

Dr Nicholas Borbon, an insurance magnate and son of landbank advocate, Praisegod 'Barebones' and John Holland, a reputable Englishman who promoted the Bank of Scotland, added their support.

Subscription (25% paid up) was launched on June 21 at Mercers' Hall, Cheapside. It was swift. £900,000 arrived within the first four days, the balance by the twelfth. Wealthy Whig merchants from the City seized the opportunity. Even the King and Queen, through the Treasury Office, committed £10,000.

Investors included treasure seekers and companies from the diverse fields of paper, linen, copper, glass, water and mining. Even, 'The Society for Improving Native Manufacture so as to keep out the Wet' and the 'Company for Sucking-Worm Engines of Mr John Lofttingh' (fire hoses) joined the euphoria.

Opposition had festered throughout the campaign. Tories demanded a competitor bank to protect the country from the predicted wave of socialism the Bank would create. Whig politicians had misgivings that the Crown might again seize control of the funds without the will of Parliament.

For years, the Stuart Kings, James & Charles had ruthlessly manipulated the nation's funds.

Assent for The Bank of England Charter emerged on 27 July 1694. In Grocers' Hall, the Old Lady, manifested by Britannia beside a mound of money, was born. She would remain there until 1734 before finally moving to Threadneedle Street. Sir John Houblon, head of a leading shipping and trading firm, became the first governor and with his deputy, Michael Godfrey, led 24 directors.

Official records show both men to be 'grocers'.

Two clauses of the Charter reflected the mood of the day. No Crown lending without Parliament's approval and no goods trading, except bills of exchange and gold and silver. The former prohibited a repeat of Stuart misappropriations and the latter pampered the jealousy of the City merchants.

A Tory Land Bank was finally promoted. Six months later, in 1696, the protege crashed and the Bank of England was finally placed to assume a mighty position.

The Charter allowed the Bank to circulate notes to the value of its capital which, at the time, was lent entirely to the Government. An overlooked clause permitted cheques, obscure Dutch devices, which were later to revolutionise banking and proliferate a plethora of country banks.

Early notes were handwritten. They could be cashed in part and endorsed 'encashable' without time limit. Two centuries later, a man produced a note for cashing and asked to keep the item as a souvenir. He was promptly told that it became the property of the Bank and so he left one penny outstanding to gain his souvenir.

Within two years a huge shock rocked the Bank. Coins from gunmetal, iron and silvered copper, damaged over time and heavily clipped, were to be withdrawn. Old coins, valued by weight, would be replaced by a new mint of face value. The Bank would lose half its money. Calling up 50% of its unpaid capital to 80%, just saved the day.

The crisis subsided, but several more loomed large.

Using salt duties for the forthcoming year as security, the Government in 1697 encouraged the Bank to raise yet more cash. This time for war in Flanders. In return for the £1,001,171 at 8% interest, the Bank of England gained a monopoly.

The famous Clause 28 declared 'no Corporation, Society, Fellowship, Company or Constitution in the nature of a bank was to be erected or established, permitted, suffered, countenanced, nor allowed during the continuance of the Bank of England'.

Anyone caught forging the Bank's currency would be sentenced to death, 'without the benefit of clergy', an exact penalty as existed for clipping or coining the King's money.

The Bank had obtained the approval of the Realm.

Though it now had a unique role, the Old Lady made an enormous mistake in not opening branches and offering countrywide access to capital. Total control of the banking business was there for the taking.

In 1707, the Government under The Act of Union, with Scotland appointed the Bank as fiscal agent for Exchequer Bills worth £1.5 million and initiated the close Treasury ties that exist today.

To prevent Joint Stock Companies encroaching the Bank's privileged Charter, an Act in 1708 prohibited any entity with more than six partners from issuing notes, payable on demand in less than six months. Though successfully frustrating opposition, it did lead to numerous small traders conducting banking business, only frequently to fail though over-ambition and recklessness.

Renewal of the Charter approached again. A South Seas frenzy and another war, with Spain this time, spawned dubious flotations. 'Salt pans for Holy Island.' 'A Wheel for Perpetual Motion.' 'A machine gun that fires round and square ammunition, round for Christian enemies-square for Turks.' 'An Undertaking of Great Advantage-which will be revealed in due course.'

The Bubble burst.

Sword Blade Bank went bust in 1712 and there was a run on the Old Lady. To stem the flow, the staff made payments in sixpences and shillings to friends who carried them round to the Bank's back door to enable the tills to be replenished.

When Bonnie Prince Charlie threatened to return with a French invasion force, it caused the first Black Friday, 6 December 1745.

Once more the coin mechanism of the employees was seen to work.

In reality, merchants meeting at Garraways Coffee House in Change Alley, Lombard Street, the future home of Barclays

Bank Plc saved the situation. They resolved to accept banknotes and use them for payment themselves.

A crushing battle at Culloden ended the Prince's aspirations. The '45 crisis abated.

In 1780, The Old Lady was nearly stormed during the Gordon Riots. 534 soldiers were despatched to defend her honour.

After the Lord Major was pushed to the ground, the Bank threatened 'if this 'arrogant behaviour persisted' it would leave Threadneedle Street for the safety of Somerset House.

She never did. She stayed steadfast in the heart of the City of London to develop, arguably, the most envied and admired reputation in the world today.

BIBLIOGRAPHY

Clapham, J. (1944). *The Bank of England a History*. Cambridge: Cambridge University Press.

Richards, R.D. (1934) *The First 50 Years of The Bank of England (1694–1744)*. Leiden: Nijhoff.

Saw, R. (1944). *The Bank of England* 1694-1944. London: Harrap.

OTHER BOOKS BY THE AUTHOR

As Good As Gold - History of Pound Sterling. ISBN 0-9534818-4-0

De La Rue Straw Hats to Global Securities. ISBN 0- 9534818-2-4

Euro History & Development. ISBN 0-9534818-1-6

Holidays 2000 – A Time Capsule. ISBN 0-9534818-7-5

Negotiate to Win! - The Introductory Edition. ISBN 0-9534818-6-7

Start Any Business (Print). ISBN 9781903467008
Start Any Business (eBook). ISBN 9781903467015

Scripophily - Historic Bond & Share Collecting. ISBN 0-9534818-5-9

The Eternal Old Lady - Bank of England. ISBN 0-9534818-3-2
The Eternal Old Lady (eBook). ISBN 9781903467152

The Green Shoots of Money (Print). ISBN 9781903467107
The Green Shoots of Money (eBook). ISBN 9781903467114

The Hitmen - Part One. ISBN 0-9534818-8-3

FORTHCOMING BOOKS BY THE AUTHOR

As Good As Gold (Print). ISBN 9781903467039
As Good As Gold (eBook). ISBN 9781903467121

Currants, Olives & Cotton (Print). ISBN 9781903467077
Currants, Olives & Cotton (eBook). ISBN 9781903467169

De La Rue (Print). ISBN 9781903467046
De La Rue (eBook). ISBN 9781903467138

Euro (Print). ISBN 9781903467053
Euro (eBook). ISBN 9781903467145

Scripophily (Print). ISBN 9781903467084
Scripophily (eBook). ISBN 9781903467176

Tail-less Cats & Three-legged Men (Print). ISBN 9781903467091
Tail-less Cats & Three-legged Men (eBook). ISBN 9781903467183

ABOUT THE AUTHOR

Ian Moncrief-Scott has over fifty years of broad business experience, mostly gained at international level, based in the UK.

As a former senior executive for a global publishing and information technology company headquartered in the USA, he has contributed to numerous client-facing procurement and outsourcing initiatives worldwide.

Ian has created and participated in numerous small businesses in the UK, Isle of Man and elsewhere.

He has also represented the Isle of Man Government Department for Enterprise in several of its business support schemes. Ian designed and delivered extensive training for its Micro Business Grant Scheme.

In recognition of his long-term service to the Department, Ian was nominated for The Queen's Award for Enterprise Promotion and awarded an official Certificate of Recognition in 2018.

Throughout his career, he has maintained an active interest in start-ups, especially those involving the financial sector.

At the turn of the millennium, several of the articles written by Ian that form this short work were originally published by the Museum of American Financial History (now the Museum of American Finance).

www.ingramcontent.com/pod-product-compliance
Lightning Source LLC
Chambersburg PA
CBHW071722080526
44588CB00012B/1870